MY FIRST BOOK OF
REPTILES &
AMPHIBIANS

by Dee Phillips

MY FIRST BOOK OF
REPTILES &
AMPHIBIANS

Copyright © **ticktock Entertainment Ltd 2008**

First published in Great Britain in 2006,

Ticktock Direct Ltd, The Pantiles Chambers, 85 High Street, Tunbridge Wells, Kent, TN1 1XP

ISBN 978 1 84696 007 9 pbk

Printed in China

9 8 7 6 5 4

A CIP catalogue record for this book is available from the British Library.

Picture Credits: Alamy; 90t. OSF; 13, 15, 17, 27, 57, 79; all other images ticktock Media Archive.

CONTENTS

Words that appear in **bold** are explained in the glossary.

MEET THE REPTILES AND AMPHIBIANS

Reptiles is the word we use to describe some of the animals that live on Earth. Snakes, tortoises, turtles, lizards, crocodiles and alligators are all reptiles. **Amphibians** are another group of animals. They mostly live in or near water. Frogs, toads, newts and salamanders are all amphibians.

In some ways, they are very similar: they are both **cold-blooded**. This means that their inside body temperature goes up and down with the air or water around them. Your body temperature stays the same on the inside, no matter how hot or cold it is.

Most reptiles and amphibians lay eggs.

But there are also differences: amphibians lay their eggs in water or under leaves and the babies, which are called larvae or tadpoles, live and breathe under water, like fish. When they get bigger, they move onto land. Another difference is that reptiles' skin is made up of **scales**, but amphibians have a smooth, moist, and sometimes warty skin.

A WORLD OF REPTILES AND AMPHIBIANS
The map on this page shows our world.

The different parts of the world are called continents. North America and Africa are both continents. Some of the animals in this book live in lots of places on just one continent. Other animals live on many different continents.

Some animals in this book only live in one country, such as Australia or Japan.

When you read about an animal in your book, see if you can find the place where they live on the map.

Can you point to the part of the world where you live?

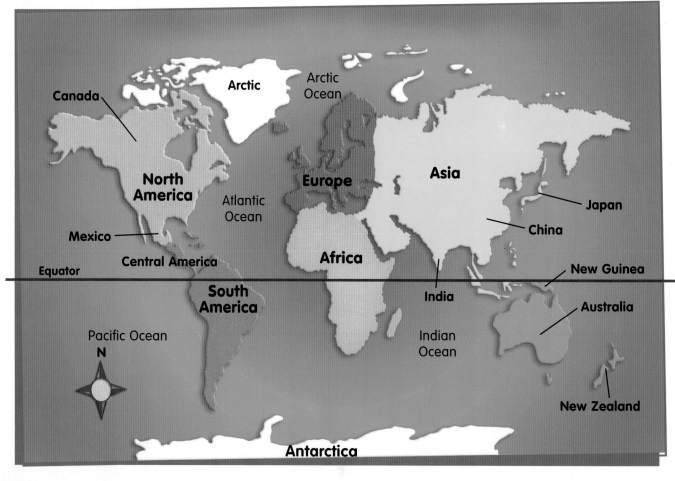

REPTILES AND AMPHIBIANS HABITATS

Some animals live in hot places, such as deserts, others live in forests or in the ocean. The different types of places where animals live are called **habitats**.

Look for these pictures in your book, and they will tell you what kind of habitat each animal lives in.

Deserts: hot, dry, sandy places where it hardly ever rains

Mountains: high, rocky places

Grasslands: dry places covered with grass

Lakes, ponds, rivers or streams

Rainforests: warm forests with lots of rain

Temperate forests: cool forests with trees that lose their leaves in winter

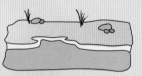

Oceans

Seashores

REPTILE AND AMPHIBIAN DIETS

Some reptiles and amphibians only eat meat, fish or bugs and spiders. Others only eat plants. Many reptiles and amphibians eat both meat and plants.

Look for these pictures in your book, and they will tell you what kind of food each animal eats.

Plants

Meat (other animals)

Fish

Bugs or spiders

ADDER

The adder is also known as a viper. It lives across parts of Europe and east Asia. It is the only **venomous snake** in north west Europe.

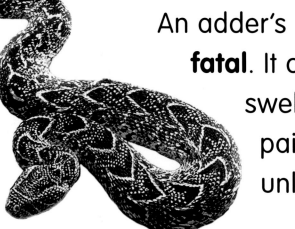

An adder's bite is rarely **fatal**. It can cause mild swelling, and is very painful, but it is unlikely to kill you.

Adders like to sunbathe. They are often seen basking on rocks.

An adder eats rats and lizards. It hunts its **prey** by chasing it or by the technique of **ambush**.

1m   2m

Adder mums only have babies every two to three years. They have litters of up to 20 young.

Adders can be grey, brown, dark red or black. Most have a zigzag line running down their back.

PYTHON

Pythons are all **snakes** which loop their bodies around their prey and squeeze to kill it. None are **venomous**.

They can swallow a deer whole.

The reticulated python (above) is the world's longest snake. Some have grown as big as 10 metres.

2m   4m   6m   8m   10m

There are 26 known
species of python.
This is a green tree python.

Python mums lay between 15 to
100 eggs. Mums keep the eggs warm
with their bodies until the eggs hatch.

BOA CONSTRICTOR

Boa constrictors get their name from the way they wrap their long bodies around their **prey**. They squeeze harder and harder until the prey cannot breathe anymore, and swallow their victims whole.

Boa constrictors are excellent swimmers. They often decide to go in water to escape the heat during summer.

Dark patches of colour help to hide boa constrictors when they are hunting for prey.

1m   2m   3m   4m   5m

Boa constrictors are very large snakes. They are adaptable creatures that can grow to frightening sizes.

ANACONDA

Anacondas live in South America.

They are the heaviest **snakes** in the world.

Some anacondas weigh 250 kilograms.

Their eyes and nostrils are on top of their heads, so they can see and breathe when they are hiding in water.

Anacondas hide from their **prey** in **shallow** water.

1m   2m   3m   4m   5m   6m   7m   8m   9m   10m

Anacondas can catch big animals, such as pigs and deer and swallow them whole.

Anacondas give birth to live baby snakes. The babies can swim and hunt just a few hours after they are born.

GABOON VIPER

Gaboon vipers are a kind of **snake**. They use their special teeth, called **fangs**, to inject **venom** into their **prey**.

Gaboon vipers have the longest fangs of any venomous snake. The fangs are about as long as your finger!

Gaboon vipers hunt for frogs, birds and other small creatures.

1m   2m

Gaboon viper mums only have babies every two to three years.

They live in **forests** in Africa.

This skin pattern helps the gaboon viper to hide among leaves.

BLACK MAMBA

As well as being the most **venomous snake**, the black mamba is probably the fastest too.

The black mamba is not actually black, but grey or brown.

It makes its home in a rock crevice or a hollow tree.

Black mambas come out during the day and feed on birds and mammals.

1m   2m   3m   4m   5m

Females lay 12 to 17 eggs in the chambers underground.

It lives in east and southern Africa.

CORAL SNAKE

These **venomous**, brightly coloured **snakes** live in warm parts of the Americas. There are about 40 species.

These colourful bands tell **predators** that the snake is poisonous and not good to eat.

They have smooth **scales**.

Coral snakes have a small head.

1m   2m

They eat other snakes and small **lizards**.

These snakes spend their time hidden in the forest and they only come out at night.

CORN SNAKE

Corn snakes live in America. They live up trees, on buildings or on the ground, hiding under logs and rocks.

Corn snakes eat rats and mice.

They taste the air with their tongues to find out if dinner is close by.

They have a Y-shaped tongue.

1m

2m

Snakes have no eyelids so their eyes stay open even when they are asleep.

Mum corn snakes lay eggs in piles of leaves. The baby snakes **hatch** from the eggs after 60 days.

EMERALD TREE BOA

Emerald tree boas live in **rainforest** trees in South America. They eat birds and small animals such as mice by strangling them.

This green skin helps the snake hide among the tree leaves.

Emerald tree boas wrap their bodies around a branch and then reach out with their heads to catch their **prey**.

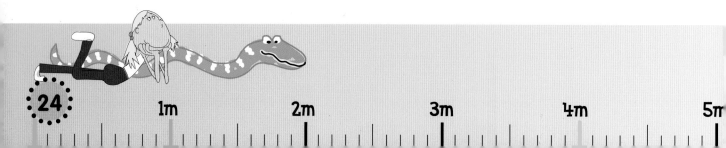

1m   2m   3m   4m   5m

The baby boas are red, yellow or orange when they are born. They start to go green when they are about one year old, like this one.

Emerald tree boas give birth to live babies.

COBRA

Cobras are **snakes** that live in lots of different **habitats** in southeast Asia and Africa. They are very **venomous**.

These markings on the back of the hood look a bit like eyes.

When the cobra meets an enemy, it rears up and spreads this hood of skin.

The spitting cobra spits venom from its **fangs**. The poison can hit **prey** two metres away.

1m   2m   3m   4m   5m

Cobras eat rats, birds, **lizards**, toads and other **snakes**.

Indian cobras lay about 12 to 20 eggs. The baby **snakes hatch** after 60 days.

SEA SNAKES

As they are cold-blooded, sea **snakes** live in warm seas. They are highly venomous. Like land snakes, sea snakes are **scaly reptiles** who shed their skin, have forked tongues and breathe air.

Sea snakes have specialised flattened tails for swimming and nostrils which close underwater.

They do not have gill slits and need to breathe air.

All sea snakes give birth to live young, apart from the banded sea snake which lays eggs on the shore.

1m   2m   3m   4m

Sea snakes are usually found in **shallow** water, where they swim about the bottom feeding on fish and eels.

RATTLESNAKE

Rattlesnakes are **venomous**. They catch their **prey** by biting them with their **fangs**.

The rattle is made of hard **scales**. It sounds like dried peas in a tin.

If a rattlesnake hears a person or animal nearby, it rattles the end of its tail to say, "Go away!"

1m   2m   3m   4m

This timber rattlesnake lives in **deserts** and hot places in America. It gives birth to live babies.

Rattlesnakes hunt **lizards**, birds and small animals such as rats.

ALLIGATOR

Alligators are very big **reptiles** that spend a lot of time in the water. They float about in **lakes**, rivers and **swamps**. There are two types of alligator: American and Chinese.

There are up to 70 teeth in their mouths.

They have webbed feet for swimming.

Alligators hunt for fish, **snakes**, turtles, **lizards** and birds. They gobble up their **prey** whole.

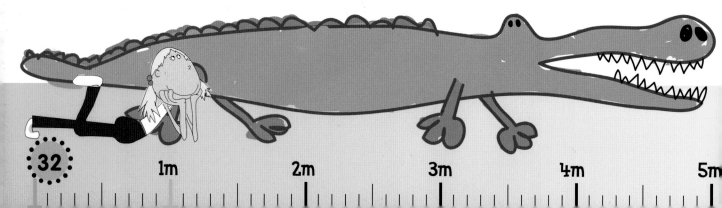

1m   2m   3m   4m   5m

The **hatchlings** call out "PEEP PEEP" to their mum as they **hatch**.

The mother carries the tiny hatchlings to the water inside her mouth.

CROCODILE

Crocodiles are huge **reptiles**. They are **predators**. Crocodiles live in Africa, Australia and southeast Asia in **lakes**, rivers and **swamps**.

Crocodiles eat lots of fish. Sometimes they catch and eat big animals such as **buffaloes**.

Mum crocodiles lay their eggs in a hole on the sandy riverbank.

They have thick skin with **scales**.

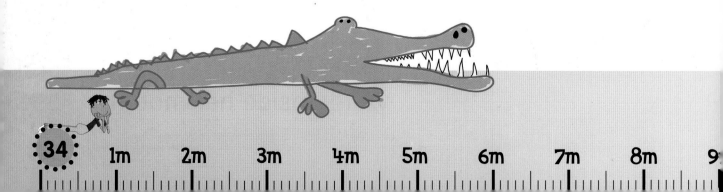

1m 2m 3m 4m 5m 6m 7m 8m 9

A crocodile egg is about twice the size of a chicken egg.

Baby crocodiles hide in their mum's mouth if there is any danger.

GHARIAL

Gharials are **reptiles** that come from the same animal family as crocodiles. They live in rivers in India and nearby countries.

Gharials have weak legs. When they are on land, they slide along on their bellies!

They have over 100 very sharp teeth in this long, thin snout.

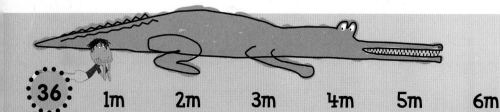

1m   2m   3m   4m   5m   6m   7m   8m   9m

Only boys have a
lump on their snout.

Gharials spend most of their time
in water. They mainly eat fish.

Mum gharials dig nest holes
away from the river. Then they
lay about 60 eggs in one go.

CAIMAN

This fierce **reptile** is another member of the crocodile family. Caimans live in Central and South America.

Mum caimans build a nest for their eggs made from leaves and plants. The nest is made either at the edge of the water or floating on the water.

They hunt at night for fish, other **reptiles**, birds and **amphibians**.

1m   2m   3m   4m   5m

Sometimes caimans share a nest. The mums work as a team guarding the nest against **predators**.

GECKO

Geckos live in warm places like **rainforests** and **deserts**. They are the only lizards that have a voice, which sounds like "gecko". This is how they got their name.

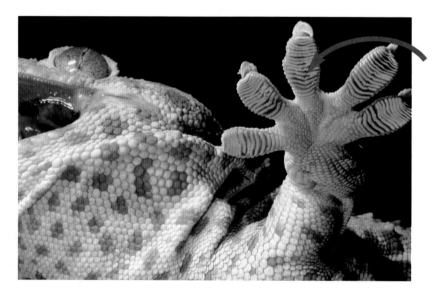

These feet can climb anything – even, smooth, slippery glass.

There are about 400 species of gecko. The largest is a tokay (like the one above).

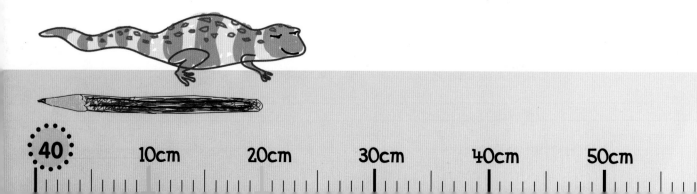

10cm   20cm   30cm   40cm   50cm   60

Geckos hunt at night for insects, but they also eat young birds, eggs and tiny mammals.

This is a Madagascan day gecko.

Most mum geckos lay eggs with soft shells. It takes up to 60 days for the eggs to **hatch**.

CHAMELEON

Chameleons are **lizards** with special skin that can change colour if they get cross or excited, and can allow them to blend in with their environment.

Its tongue shoots out so fast, you cannot see it.
It is longer than the chameleon's body.

This tail can hold onto branches.

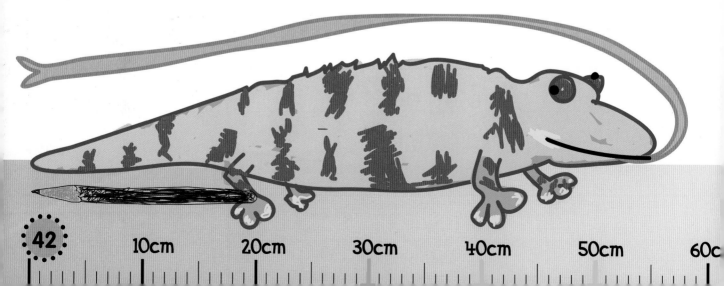

10cm   20cm   30cm   40cm   50cm   60c

This is a Jackson's chameleon. It lives in east Africa and Hawaii.

One eye can look forward, while the other eye is looking backward.

IGUANA

Iguanas are a kind of large **lizard**. They live in the **rainforests**, **deserts** and one type lives by the sea.

Iguanas vary in colour from green to brown to yellow.

If attacked, the iguana uses its tail like a whip.

They use their powerful legs to swim and climb trees.

1m   2m

A female iguana will dig a **shallow** trench in moist soil in which she will lay 20 to 70 eggs. Then she will cover the eggs with soil.

Iguanas mainly eat plants, insects, worms and small animals.

BEARDED DRAGON

The bearded dragon is a kind of **lizard**. It lives in **forests** and hot, dry places in Australia.

A frill of skin – a bit like a beard.

If a **predator** comes near, the dragon puffs up its beard and opens its mouth wide to look scary.

1m   2m

They sit on branches, or sometimes on fences, keeping watch over their **territory**.

Bearded dragons eat bugs, plants, fruit and flowers. They live on the ground and in trees.

Mums lay their eggs in sandy ground. The babies **hatch** out on their own.

FRILLED LIZARD

Frilled **lizards** live in **forests** in Australia. They live up in the trees, but search for food on the ground.

Frilled lizards eat bugs and other smaller lizards.

When a **predator** comes close, the frilled lizard opens up its big frill of skin and hisses to make itself seem scary. Then it quickly runs up a tree to escape.

20cm   40cm   60cm   70cm   80cm

The frill folds down over the lizard's shoulders.

Mum frilled lizards lay about eight eggs at a time.

THORNY DEVIL LIZARD

Thorny devils are **lizards** that live in hot **deserts** in Australia. They are strange, shy creatures.

The thorny devil lizard has spikes all over its body. The spikes protect it from **predators**.

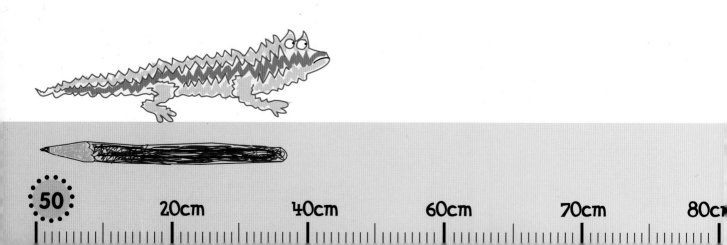

20cm   40cm   60cm   70cm   80cm

Thorny devils eat ants. They lick them up with their tongues – one ant at a time.

They eat thousands of ants in one meal, so dinner takes a long time.

Mum thorny devil lizards lay their eggs in underground **burrows**.

THAI WATER DRAGON

Thai water dragons are large **lizards** that live in southeast Asia. They live in **forests** near **lakes** and streams.

If a **predator** comes close, the lizard escapes into the water. The tail helps the lizard move through water.

Thai water dragons spend time on the ground and in trees.

Their long toes with claws are good for climbing.

1m 2m 3m 4m

Mums lay eggs in **burrows** and cover them with earth and leaves.

Thai water dragons eat small animals, such as other lizards. Sometimes they eat plants.

BLUE-TONGUED SKINK

This large **lizard** lives in various different **habitats** in Australia.

It has a wide head.

It has a chubby body.

It has short legs.

In the daytime, the blue tongued skink sunbathes and looks for snails, bugs, fruit, flowers and berries to eat.

Baby skinks are ten centimetres long when they are born.

1m

2m

If a **predator** attacks, the skink hisses and rolls out its long, bright blue tongue to scare away the other animal.

At night, it sleeps in a log or pile of dead leaves.

55

GILA MONSTER

Gila monsters are big, **venomous**, slow-moving **lizards**. They live in **deserts** in America and Mexico.

They have scaly skin that looks like small beads.

Gila monsters store fat in their tails. Their bodies use up the fat for energy when there is no food available.

Gila monsters eat rats, birds, frogs, other lizards and eggs.

When they bite their **prey**, venom comes out of their teeth.

20cm   40cm   60cm   70cm   80cm

Baby gila monsters are ten centimetres long when they **hatch** from their eggs.

KOMODO DRAGON

The giant komodo dragon is the biggest of all the **lizards**. Komodo dragons live on **islands** near southeast Asia.

They can smell food from up to ten kilometres away and often eat other animals' leftover meat.

The komodo has a deadly bite from the **poisonous** bacteria in its saliva.

They have a forked tongue.

1m   2m   3m   4m   5m

Mum dragons dig out large **burrows** in sandy ground for their eggs.

When the babies **hatch**, they live up in the trees to stay away from **predators**.

SLOW WORM

Slow worms look like **snakes** but they are actually **lizards** with no legs. (Lizards have eyelids; snakes do not.) When it is cold in winter, slow worms **hibernate**.

They eat bugs, worms and slugs.

Slow worms live in fields and on farmland across Europe and west Asia.

20cm   40cm   60cm   70cm   80c

If a **predator** grabs a slow worm's tail, it breaks off. But it will soon grow back.

Mum slow worms give birth to live babies.

TUATARA

The tuatara looks like a **lizard**, but is not. They are found on two small groups of islands off the coast of New Zealand.

Tuatara eggs take up to a year to develop inside the female's body and take up to 14 months to **hatch**.

Tuataras live a very long time (possibly over 100 years).

1m   2m

They live in burrows and
mainly come out at night.

They eat beetles, crickets, small **lizards**
and occasionally bird eggs and chicks.

GALAPAGOS TORTOISE

Tortoises are reptiles with shells. Galapagos tortoises are the biggest tortoises in the world. They live on **islands** near South America.

They like to munch on plants, grass and **cacti**. They also like to sunbathe and relax in muddy puddles.

Like other tortoises, they can pull their limbs and head inside their shell.

1m   2m   3m

Mums dig a nest in sandy ground. They lay eggs the size of tennis balls.

Tortoises are related to turtles, who live in the ocean, and terrapins, who live in freshwater.

SEA TURTLE

Sea turtles are swimming **reptiles** with shells. There are many different types of sea turtle and they live in oceans all around the world.

Most sea turtles eat meat, but the green turtle, like this one, lives on plants.

All sea turtle species are endangered or threatened.

1m   2m   2m

Mum turtles crawl up on to a beach and dig a hole in the sand for their eggs.

When the eggs **hatch**, the baby turtles have to run to the sea before they are spotted by **predators**.

SNAPPING TURTLE

This fierce **reptile** lives in **lakes**, ponds, streams and rivers in parts of North and South America.

The snapping turtle has no teeth. It uses its hard, hooky beak to slice at **prey**.

The turtle's head cannot fit into its shell so it bites at **predators** to protect itself.

Mums dig nest holes on land with their back legs. They lay 20 to 30 eggs, then go back to their pond or river.

20cm   40cm   60cm   70cm   80c

Snapping turtles eat frogs, toads, **snakes**, small animals and plants.

They hide, buried in underwater mud, ready to jump out on their prey.

TERRAPINS

Terrapins are freshwater turtles that live in swampy waters, **lakes** and rivers. They spend much of their lives in the water.

This is a helmeted terrapin. Like all terrapins, it eats meat and catches most of its **prey** in the water.

Some terrapins can spend the winter underwater, buried in mud.

10cm 20cm 30cm 40cm 50c

Terrapins, like this diamondback terrapin, lay eggs on land, cover them up, and then leave the **hatchlings** to fend for themselves.

They eat fish, water insects, insect **larvae** and snails.

PAINTED TURTLE

The painted turtle lives in North America, and it is also called a painted terrapin. It spends most of its time in the water, but suns itself while lying on a rock, on a log or the shore.

They live in ponds, **lakes**, marshes and slow-moving rivers.

In the wild, they can live between 5 to 10 years.

20cm   40cm   60cm   70cm   80cm

During very cold weather, northern painted turtles **hibernate** by burying themselves in the mud.

Female painted turtles lay 5 to 10 eggs in a shallow pit that they dig with their hind legs. They then abandon them, and the eggs **hatch** in about 10 to 11 weeks.

EUROPEAN COMMON FROG

The European common frog is the most common frog in northern Europe. It lives close to **lakes**, ponds, rivers and streams.

Frog mums lay thousands of eggs in one go. The eggs are called frogspawn. They look like a big clump of jelly.

The baby frogs are called tadpoles. They hatch after about two weeks, if the weather is warm enough.

10cm   20cm   30cm   40cm   50c

Frogs catch bugs to eat on their long, sticky tongues.

They spend most of their lives on land, and return to the water to breed.

TREE FROG

Tree frogs live in Australia, New Guinea, Europe America and Asia. There are many different types of tree frogs.

Tree frogs have sticky pads on their fingers and toes to help them climb trees, like this red-eyed tree frog.

These frogs usually come out at night looking for bugs to ea

10cm   20cm   30cm   40cm   50cm

Giant tree frogs are the largest type of tree frog. They can grow to about 12 cm.

Mum frogs lay their eggs in water – the White's tree frog lays up to 3,000 eggs in one go.

HORNED FROG

There are many types of horned frog. This large, fat species lives in the rainforest in South America and Asia.

The Asian horned frog has a huge head, with two horn-like protrusions above its eyes which deter **predators**.

Females can lay up to 1,000 eggs. They wrap these around aquatic plants.

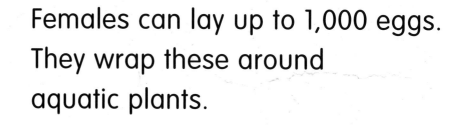

10cm   20cm   30cm   40cm   50c

Horned frogs
catch lizards,
mice and
other frogs
by burying
themselves in
the ground and
pouncing as
they pass by.

This is a
Chacoan
horned frog.

NORTH AMERICAN BULLFROG

North American bullfrogs are big, greedy frogs that live in America.

They eat other frogs, **reptiles**, birds, fish – anything they can swallow.

Bullfrogs live in **lakes**, ponds and streams.

They can leap two metres with their long, strong back legs.

10cm   20cm   30cm   40cm   50cm

The round circles behind the eyes are the frog's eardrums.

Dad bullfrogs protect their **territory** from other frogs by chasing them, having wrestling fights and making loud noises.

POISON DART FROG

Poison dart frogs live in **rainforests** in central America. Native people use their poison on arrows and darts when they go hunting.

When the eggs hatch, they carry the tadpoles on their backs to tree holes filled with water.

Poison dart frogs can be red, blue or green.

Green poison dart frog mums lay 5 to 13 eggs in water-filled tree holes.

10cm   20cm   30cm   40cm   50c

The bright colours are a defence mechanism.
They warn **predators** that the frog is **poisonous.**

EUROPEAN COMMON TOAD

The European common toad is one of Europe's most common amphibians. It also lives in parts of Asia and Africa.

They spend the day in cool, damp places. They mainly come out at night, looking for bugs and slugs to eat.

Mum toads lay long strings of eggs in ponds.

10cm   20cm   30cm   40cm   50c

Toads have special places behind their eyes which make nasty-tasting stuff that stops **predators** eating them.

FIRE SALAMANDER

The fire salamander is an **amphibian**. It lives in **forests** in Africa, Europe and west Asia.

This yellow and black skin tells **predators** that the salamander has **poison** on its skin and is bad to eat.

When they grow up, they live on land and breathe air like humans.

10cm   20cm   30cm   40cm   50cm

Fire salamanders eat worms, slugs and bugs.

Baby fire salamanders are called **larvae**. They live in ponds and streams and can breathe underwater just like fish.

JAPANESE GIANT SALAMANDER

Japanese giant salamanders are the biggest **amphibians** in the world.

They live in cold **mountain** streams and rivers in Japan.

Japanese giant salamanders eat many different foods, including crabs, bugs, mice and fish.

They can go for weeks without eating if there is no food.

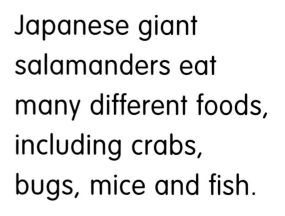

1m   2m

Females lay about 500 eggs in long strings, in holes dug by males.

Dads guard the eggs until they **hatch**. They are very fierce if **predators** come near the eggs.

MUDPUPPY

Mudpuppies are a type of salamander. They live in freshwater, in southern Canada, central and eastern USA. It remains aquatic for life.

The Mudpuppy has two pairs of limbs, each with a four-toed foot.

Female mudpuppies dig a nest under rocks and logs and guard their eggs until they **hatch**, about two months later.

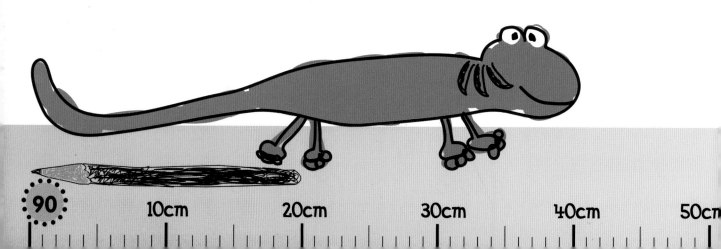

10cm   20cm   30cm   40cm   50cm

Mudpuppies have feathery, external gills.

They are brown, grey or black, usually with black spots or blotches.

GREAT CRESTED NEWT

Newts look like **lizards**, but they are **amphibians**. Great crested newts live near ponds and **lakes**, in Europe. Adult newts spend the summer or entire year in water.

In the daytime they hide under logs or stones. At night they look for food – tadpoles, worms and bug **larvae**.

Male great crested newts have a jagged crest.

10cm   20cm   30cm   40cm   50c

Mum newts lay
two to three eggs
every day for
about five months.

The **larvae hatch**
out and live in
the water until
they become
grown-ups.

They wrap their eggs in
leaves and hide them
among water plants.

Glossary

ambush A surprise attack by someone lying in a hidden position.

amphibians Animals that spend part of their time in water and part on land; amphibians lay their eggs in water. Frogs, toads, newts and salamanders are amphibians.

bark The tough, outer covering of tree trunks and tree branches.

buffaloes Big, plant-eating wild animals that look a bit like cows. Buffaloes can be two metres tall.

burrows Holes or tunnels that animals dig as homes.

cacti Plants that have spikes instead of leaves; they often live in hot dry places such as deserts.

deserts Places where hardly any rain falls; many lizards and snakes live in deserts, even though they are hot, dry places.

fangs Very sharp teeth; snakes' fangs are hollow (like drinking straws) and are used to inject poison into their prey.

fatal Causing death.

forests Places where there are lots of trees.

geckos Small reptiles with four legs and a tail; they are a kind of lizard; they have special feet that help them to climb up slippery things like glass.

grasslands Dry places covered with grass, with very few bushes or trees.

habitats Different types of places around the world, such as forests, deserts and grasslands.

hatch To be born by breaking out of an egg.

hatchlings The name for the babies of some reptiles; they are called hatchlings because they hatch from eggs.

hibernate To spend the winter sleeping in a burrow (or other warm, safe place) while there is not much food around.

islands Small areas of land completely surrounded by water.

lakes Large areas of inland water.

larvae The name for the babies of creatures such as bugs and newts; these animals start as eggs; they hatch out as larvae and then grow and change into grown-ups.

lizards Reptiles with scaly skin and legs. Some

lizards are tiny; others such as the komodo dragon are huge.

mountains Large, rocky areas of land that are much higher than the surrounding area.

poison Nasty stuff that can make a person or animal very ill and even kill them; some animals have poison inside their bodies that they use for killing their prey.

poisonous The word we use to describe something that can kill when eaten.

predators Animals that live by hunting and eating other animals.

prey An animal that is hunted by another animal for food.

rainforests Warm, jungle-like forests with very tall trees and lots of plants and animals.

reptiles Animals such as snakes, lizards, tortoises and turtles. They are cold-blooded and have scaly skin. Some reptiles lay eggs and some give birth to live babies.

scales Tough, flat sections of skin on the bodies of reptiles. They are made of the same stuff as your fingernails and toenails.

sea sponges Very simple ocean animals; they live attached to something such as a rock on the seabed; you might have some soft, yellow, natural sea sponge in your bathroom.

shallow When something, such as water, is not very deep.

snakes Long, thin reptiles with scaly skin and no legs.

swamps Places where there is lots of water or mud, and the ground is soft, wet and very squishy.

territory The area where an animal lives. Animals guard their territories to stop other animals eating the food in that area.

venomous Producing a poisonous fluid injected by a bite or sting.

Index